Guerrilla marketing

The secret weapons for those who want to spend little
and have a lot of results

Copyright

"Be a fish out of water in the ocean of conventional marketing."

"Boldness is Guerrilla Marketing's secret ammunition."

"Don't wait for opportunities, create them with your own hands."

"Creativity is the soul of Guerrilla Marketing, and courage is its driving force."

"Think beyond the limits, because that's where innovation flourishes."

"Guerrilla Marketing is the art of surprising and delighting."

"Be memorable or be forgotten. It's your choice."

A brief introduction

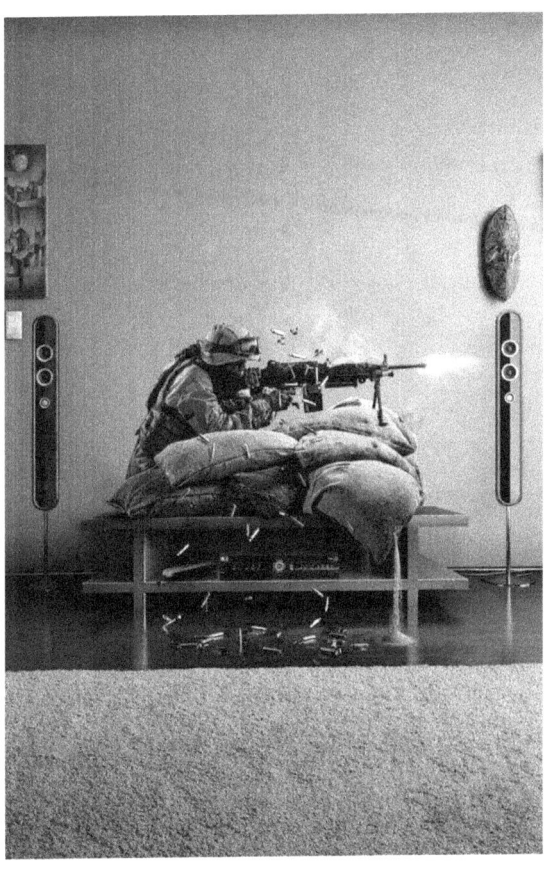

But after all, what is Guerrilla Marketing?

Imagine an army of small businesses, entrepreneurs and marketers, all united in one mission: to win the attention and heart of the target audience, even without the huge resources of large corporations. This is the essence of Guerrilla Marketing.

Unlike traditional marketing, which often depends on huge budgets and massive advertisements, Guerrilla Marketing is committed to creativity, innovation and the intelligent use of available resources. It is an approach that defies convention, seeks to break down barriers and create emotional connections with the audience.

In the current business scenario, where competition is fierce and public attention is disputed on several fronts, Guerrilla

Marketing has become a powerful weapon. It allows even the smallest companies with limited budgets to compete effectively, gaining visibility and engagement.

What makes Guerrilla Marketing so special is its ability to go beyond traditional means of outreach. It leverages public spaces, events, social media and other platforms to create unique and memorable experiences. These unexpected and surprising actions can have a lasting impact, making brands stand out amid the noise of the market.

In addition, the Guerrilla Marketing is deeply rooted in understanding and respecting the target audience. By knowing their wants, needs and behaviors, it is possible to create highly segmented and personalized campaigns, increasing audience relevance and engagement.

The term "guerrilla marketing" was popularized by Jay Conrad Levinson in his book "Guerrilla Marketing", published in 1984.

While Levinson didn't completely invent the strategy, he helped popularize it and turn it into one of the most widely used marketing tactics today.

The idea of using creative and unconventional strategies to obtain marketing results existed before, but Levinson was responsible for defining the principles and techniques that make up guerrilla marketing.

Jay Conrad Levinson got the idea for guerrilla marketing from observing the strategies used by the Vietnamese during the Vietnam War.

He noticed that, even with few resources, the Vietnamesecould win battles against a stronger and better equipped army. Levinson applied this same idea to marketing, creating an approach that sought to achieve marketing objectives with minimal resources and maximum creativity.

He believed that guerrilla marketing was the answer for small businesses that didn't have massive advertising budgets but still needed to find ways to stand out in the marketplace and achieve their goals.

From then on, the concept of guerrilla marketing became popular and became one of the main strategies used by companies of different sizes and segments.

Who are we going to target?

Understanding your target audience is essential to the success of any marketing campaign. It's like looking through a clear and sharp lens that allows us to see who are the people who really matter to our business. In this chapter, we'll explore the importance of identifying and understanding your target audience, providing you with the tools you need to create effective campaigns.

The first question we must ask is: who are the people we are trying to reach? The target audience is the specific group of individuals who are interested in what our brand or product has to offer. To identify it, we need to go beyond superficial demographics and dive into the motivations, needs and desires that drive these people.

An effective way to understand your target audience is to conduct research and collect relevant data. We may use questionnaires, interviews and market analysis to obtain valuable information. We need to find out what they are looking for, what their challenges are, how they behave and what their preferences are. By knowing your values, interests and lifestyle, we can create a genuine and relevant connection.

Pay attention to trends and changes in consumer behavior. The world evolves, and as it evolves, we must keep up with these transformations to adjust our marketing strategies accordingly.

Social media, for example, is a valuable source of information about target audiences. They allow us to observe how people communicate, what they share and what they expect from brands.

Another aspect is segmentation. By breaking the target audience down into smaller, more specific segments, we can create personalized messages that resonate more powerfully. We may group people based on characteristics such as age, gender, interests, purchasing behavior and geographic location. This allows us to adapt our campaigns according to the needs of each segment.

However, understanding the target audience goes beyond data and statistics. It's about developing empathy and genuine understanding. We need to put ourselves in our customers' shoes, understand their concerns and desires.

How to think unconventionally

Guerrilla Marketing offers a perfect platform to break down barriers and challenge convention, allowing you to create truly memorable campaigns.

Thinking outside the box is like opening a door to a new universe. It's about breaking with pre-established ideas and exploring new ways to communicate your message. Your goal is to stand out amidst the noise of the market, capturing your audience's imagination and leaving a lasting mark.

Creativity is the spark that lights the fire of innovation. It is the ability to find unique, out-of-the-box solutions to the challenges you face. In Guerrilla Marketing, it is the key to creating impactful and surprising actions that generate engagement and arouse curiosity.

But how to develop creative ideas that actually work? First, you need to free your mind from limitations. Open yourself up to new perspectives, ask challenging questions and explore different angles. Unleash your imagination and allow yourself to dream big. Think of what's impossible and then find a way to make it possible.

Connect seemingly disconnected ideas. Immerse yourself in different areas of knowledge, be inspired by different industries and cultures. Look for insights in unexpected places and find ways to apply them to your Guerrilla Marketing context. These surprising connections can generate truly innovative ideas.

Remember to involve your team in brainstorming sessions. Collaboration and diversity of thought are powerful sources of inspiration. By bringing together brilliant minds and different perspectives, you can foster an environment of collective creativity, where ideas flow freely and transform into incredible concepts.

Don't be afraid to take risks and experiment. In Guerrilla Marketing, it is necessary to leave the comfort zone and embrace uncertainty. Test new approaches, venture into uncharted territory and learn from the results. Sometimes the best ideas are born from bold and daring experiments.

Creativity must beenhanced with practice. Keep up to date with trends and the latest news in the market. Seek inspiration from Guerrilla Marketing success stories and find your own unique style.

surprise and shock

Surprise and shock are geared toward grabbing audience attention and creating immediate impact. Here are some ways to use unexpected and provocative elements:

Visual shock: Create ads or graphic pieces with surprising and impactful images. Use vibrant colors, strong contrasts, and out-of-the-ordinary visuals to catch the audience's eye.

Provocative messages: Use direct, bold messages that encourage the public to reflect. Break taboos, challenge established beliefs and create controversy to generate impact and spark curiosity.

Bold Prints: Design t-shirts, stickers or other products with provocative and unexpected prints. Be creative and use powerful phrases, striking symbols or intriguing designs.

Digital Guerrilla: Use online strategies to surprise the public. Create viral content, take actions on social media that defy expectations and promote unusual interactions that generate buzz.

Surprise Events: Hold interventions or unannounced events in public places. Make a splash with performances, flash mobs or creative demonstrations to surprise and shock those around you.

Unconventional advertising: Use alternative means to convey your message, such as projections on buildings, interactive billboards or even graffiti in strategic spaces. Awakening the public's curiosity is essential.

Shattering Expectations: Surprise audiences by challenging your industry's conventions. Do something unexpected, innovative and out of the ordinary, showing a new side of your brand.

The goal is to make a lasting impact and get people to remember your brand. However, it's important to strike a balance between shock and the message you want to convey, to ensure the approach is effective and in line with your brand values.

Low budget, maximum impact

Having a small budget does not mean you are at a disadvantage.

In fact, it's an opportunity to be even more creative and innovative. The key is to find smart ways to use your resources strategically for maximum impact.

One of the most effective strategies is to leverage digital and online platforms. With a smaller investment compared to traditional channels, you can reach a broad and highly targeted audience. Use social networks, blogs, email marketing and other online tools to create a direct relationship with your target audience, spreading your message in an economical and targeted way.

Another approach is content marketing. By creating relevant, informative and quality content, you can position your brand as an authority in your industry. This doesn't require a huge financial investment, but rather an investment of time and dedication to research, write and promote your content.

With a well-planned strategy, your content can reach a vast and engaged audience, generating visibility and interest in your brand.

Don't forget about strategic partnerships. Seek alliances with other brands, influencers or online communities that have similar values and target audiences to yours. Together, you can develop joint campaigns, share resources and reach a wider audience. These partnerships can result in greater exposure for your brand, without the need for large financial investments.

Take advantage of high traffic locations, such as parks, squares and events, to create unique and memorable experiences. Use your creativity to grab people's attention and generate buzz around your brand. These unexpected actions can have a significant impact, piquing curiosity and generating interest in your product or service.

And don't underestimate the power of word of mouth. Deliver excellent customer service, create positive experiences, and turn your customers into brand advocates. The power of personal recommendations is immense and can fuel your growth even with limited financial resources.

Don't forget to measure and analyze the results of your strategies. Use data analysis tools to track how your campaigns are performing and adjust your approach as needed. This will allow you to target your resources more efficiently, focusing on the strategies that bring the best results.

An inspiring example is the case of the shoe company TOMS. Rather than spend a large amount of money on traditional advertising, TOMS opted for a cause marketing strategy. They created an innovative business model in which, for every pair of shoes sold, a pair was donated to a needy child. This differentiated approach generated an emotional connection with consumers, who felt part of a greater cause when purchasing a product from the brand. The result? TOMS achieved global success and became a benchmark in the footwear market, with a loyal and engaged customer base.

Another notable case is the campaign "Dumb Ways to Die" (Stupid Ways to Die) of the Melbourne subway, in Australia. With a limited budget, they created a fun and engaging animated video that warned of the risks of dangerous behavior in subway stations. The video went viral on social media and conquered the public, becoming a global success.

In addition, the campaign expanded to other formats such as mobile games and licensed products.

The result has been a massive awareness of metro safety and a significant increase in the adoption of safe behaviors by users.

Another striking example is the campaign by sportswear brand Under Armour, titled "I Will What I Want".

With a modest budget, they developed a powerful campaign that highlighted the stories of inspiring women who defied convention and achieved their goals in sport. Utilizing social media and digital content, the campaign became a viral success, generating engagement and creating an emotional connection with the audience.

Under Armor's smart strategy has given the brand visibility and strengthened its image as a supporter of female empowerment.

These successful cases demonstrate that it is possible to achieve significant results even with limited resources.

Creativity, innovation and a strategic approach are key to maximizing the impact of your marketing. By telling engaging stories, connecting with your target audience's emotions and leveraging digital platforms, you can reach a broad and engaged audience, even without large financial investments.

Remember that Guerrilla Marketing is not just about money, it's about creativity, daring and understanding your target audience.

By seeking inspiration from successful cases and adapting strategies to your brand's needs, you'll be on the right track to achieve amazing results, regardless of the size of your budget.

Viral campaigns: Strategies for creating shareable content and achieving high visibility

One of the most powerful techniques for creating viral campaigns is storytelling. Telling engaging stories is a proven way to capture audience attention and encourage sharing.

By creating content that awakens emotions, connections and identification with the audience, you will be creating a solid foundation for sharing and propagating your message.

Speaking of Storytelling, I couldn't forget about creating surprising and impactful content. By offering something out of the ordinary that surprises and delights your audience, you increase the chances that people will want to share that experience with their friends, family, and followers. It could be an inspiring video, a stunning image or an innovative idea that makes an immediate impact.

By creating content related to trending topics, you increase the likelihood that people will want to share and join the conversation.

Keep an eye out for social media trends, relevant news and popular events, and find creative ways to incorporate these elements into your content.

Emotion is one of the main triggers for sharing content. By eliciting positive emotions such as joy, surprise, inspiration or humor, you increase the chances that people will want to share your message with others. Develop content that touches your audience's heart, whether it's through heartwarming stories, funny videos or inspiring messages.

Also, invest in the visual quality of your content. Attractive images and videos have greater potential for sharing on social media. Use striking visuals, well-designed graphics, and an attractive design to make your content more engaging and shareable.

An advanced technique for increasing reach is the strategic use of influencers.

Partnering with influential people in your niche market can boost your campaign's visibility. By engaging relevant influencers, you reach a wider audience and increase the chances that your content will be shared by a significant number of people.

Make it easy to share your content. Make sure your campaign has visible and functional share buttons across multiple social media platforms. Encourage your audience to share by offering incentives like freebies, discounts, or the chance to enter exclusive contests.

"When it comes to creating viral campaigns, one thing is certain: there is no magic formula. Viral campaigns are not an exact science, but a combination of strategy, creativity and a touch of luck. They are like colorful butterflies that fly freely, defying predictions and surprising everyone.

You have to understand that the success of a viral campaign cannot be completely controlled. Even with a well-planned strategy and impeccable execution, there's no guarantee it will become a viral phenomenon. But that doesn't mean we should give up or limit ourselves.

Viral campaigns are like an invitation to the unknown, a journey full of uncertainties and endless possibilities. They remind us that sometimes it is necessary to take risks, experiment and defy convention in order to achieve the extraordinary.

There are no hard and fast rules when it comes to creating a viral campaign. What works for one brand may not work for another. You have to be willing to think outside the box, embrace the unexpected and adapt to the constant changes in the digital world.

But even in the face of this unpredictability, there are some principles that can increase our chances of success. Authenticity is one of them. People are increasingly looking for genuine connections and real stories. By creating authentic and relevant content, you are building a solid foundation for sharing.

Another important principle is to understand your target audience. Knowing their wants, needs, and values is essential to creating content that resonates with them. After all, it's the people who share, comment and drive your campaign's reach.

Creativity is the driving force of a viral campaign. It is necessary to dare, surprise and innovate. Think outside the box, experiment with different formats, tell engaging stories, and use captivating visuals. Originality and creativity are the fuel for your message to spread quickly.

BCC technique

Let's explore the CCO (Creativity, Context and Boldness) technique for guerrilla marketing campaigns. This strategic approach combines essential elements to create impactful and memorable campaigns that stand out in the competitive landscape. Get ready to dive into this technique and find out how to apply it successfully.

Creativity: Creativity is at the heart of the OCC technique. At this stage, it is essential to think outside the box and explore innovative ideas. Look for original and different solutions to stand out from the competition. Ask yourself: How can I surprise my target audience? How can I get my message across in a unique and memorable way? Use creative assets such as striking visual concepts, clever wordplay or unconventional approaches to grab attention.

Context: Context is critical to the success of a guerrilla marketing campaign. It's important to understand the environment your campaign will run in and adapt your message to connect with your target audience in a relevant way. Consider where, when, and audience characteristics your campaign will launch. How does your message fit the context? How can you relate to your audience's experiences and interests? By creating a contextualized campaign, you increase your chances of capturing attention and generating engagement.

Audacity: Audacity is the element that differentiates a guerrilla campaign from conventional marketing strategies.

Don't be afraid to take risks, challenge convention and be irreverent. Be bold in your ideas and how you execute them.

Create impactful moments that generate curiosity, surprise or even shock. Boldness is what allows your campaign to stand out and create a lasting impact in the minds of your audience.

The CCO technique for guerrilla marketing campaigns is a strategic approach that combines creativity, context and boldness.

By applying this technique, you will be creating differentiated campaigns that stand out from the competition and generate a significant impact on your target audience.

Remember to adapt the technique to your brand characteristics, your target audience and campaign objectives.

With this approach, you'll be ready to surprise, engage, and grab your audience's attention in a memorable way.

Risks and Precautions: Important considerations when running guerrilla campaigns to avoid potential problems.

While guerrilla marketing can be an exciting strategy, use it with caution and carefully consider potential problems that may arise along the way.

I'm going to explore some important considerations to help you avoid problems and ensure the successful execution of your guerrilla campaign.

Know the laws and regulations: Before starting a guerrilla campaign, it is essential to know the laws and regulations related to marketing and advertising.

Make sure you comply with local regulations, avoiding actions that could result in legal problems or damage to your brand reputation.

Please be aware of restrictions regarding intellectual property, misuse of trademarks and trespassing on private property.

Consider your target audience: When planning your campaign, consider your target audience's sensibilities and preferences. What may seem creative and impactful to some may be offensive or inappropriate to others.

Keep your audience's values, culture, and demographics in mind when creating your content. Do a careful analysis to avoid any kind of alienation or negative reaction.

Assess potential negative impacts: While well-executed guerrilla campaigns can yield positive results, it is important to consider potential negative impacts.

Ask yourself: could my campaign damage my brand image?

Could it cause discomfort or excessive disturbance?

Carefully assess the risks involved and be prepared to deal with any unintended consequences.

Keep safety in mind: If your campaign involves activities in the physical world, such as public facilities or interventions, consider the safety of everyone involved. Make sure you obtain the necessary permits, take proper precautions, and ensure that all security measures are followed. Safety is key to preventing accidents and ensuring that your campaign is well received by the public.

Be prepared for feedback: Guerrilla campaigns often generate intense engagement and reactions. Be prepared for feedback, whether positive or negative. Monitor social media, respond to comments, and be ready to deal with potential criticism.

Be open to dialogue and use feedback as an opportunity to learn and improve your future strategies.

Timing and seasonal opportunities

In a world in constant motion, it is critical to know how to take advantage of timing and seasonal opportunities when planning your guerrilla marketing campaigns.

The ability to identify and capitalize on events, anniversaries, and opportune moments can significantly boost your campaign's success.

One of the keys to an effective guerrilla campaign is being in tune with your surroundings.

Seasonal events such as holidays, festivals, major awards or anniversaries provide an excellent opportunity to create relevant and impactful campaigns. These moments capture the audience's attention and generate strong engagement.

When leveraging seasonal events, understanding the context and expectations of your target audience is essential. Carefully consider how these events are celebrated, what the trends are, and how your brand can authentically and creatively connect to them.

Think of innovative ways to integrate seasonal themes into your message and make your campaign truly memorable.

In addition to seasonal events, opportune moments can arise in the midst of unexpected situations or emerging trends.

Be aware of the social, cultural and technological changes taking place around you. Opportunities can come suddenly, and being prepared to act quickly can make all the difference.

However, I emphasize that proper timing requires sensitivity and common sense. Make sure your campaign is relevant to the moment and not perceived as opportunistic or insensitive.

Take into account the feelings and emotions of those involved in the event or situation.

To take full advantage of seasonal opportunities, be prepared and plan ahead.

Conduct research, create an event calendar, and develop creative strategies that align with your brand personality.

Stay flexible and open to adjustments should last-minute changes arise.

Remember that perfect timing is a combination of preparation, acumen and efficient execution. Be proactive, be aware of events and opportune moments and be agile in your response.

success stories

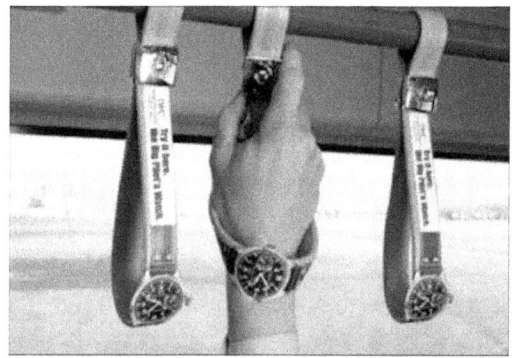

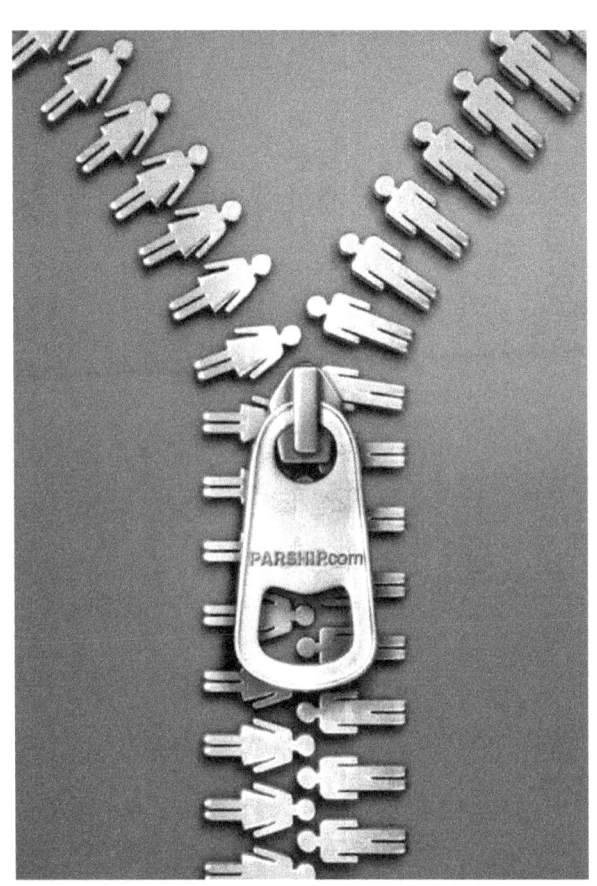

" 자연을 쓰고 계십니다. "

GREENPEACE

당신의 연필 끝에서 숲이 살아납니다.

kobaco
한국방송광고공사

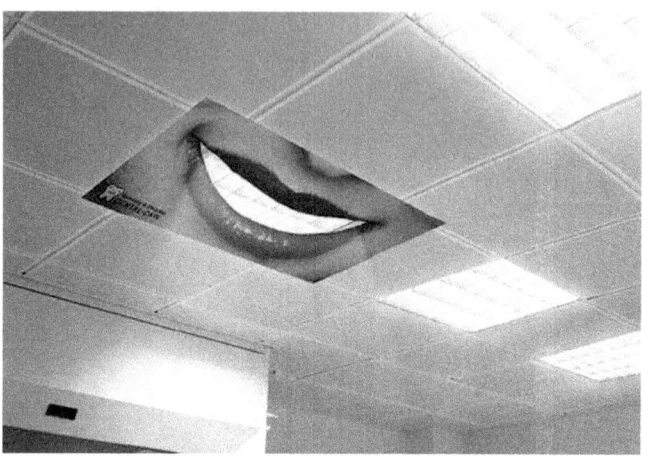

FOI ASSIM QUE A NIVEA ANUNCIOU SEU CREME CONTRA CELULITE.

I'm your father.

Dad, tell me about the ´60s again!

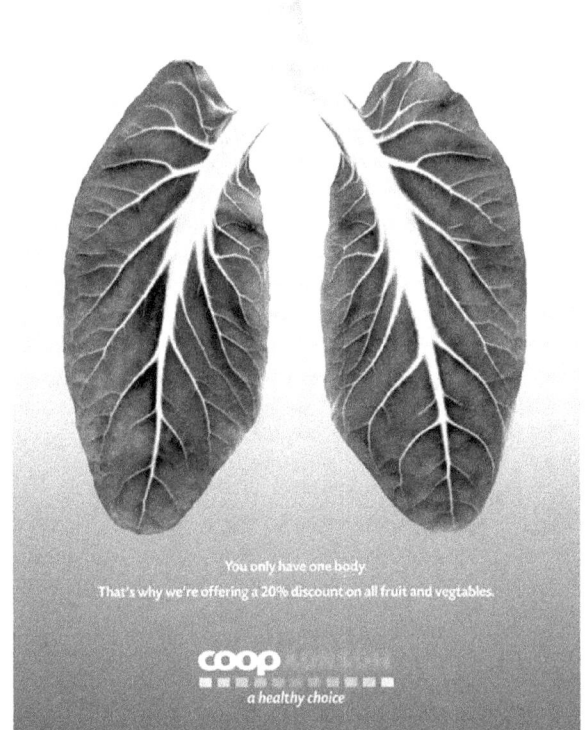

You only have one body.
That's why we're offering a 20% discount on all fruit and vegtables.

coop
a healthy choice

IN THE HANDS OF A CYBERCRIMINAL, A COMPUTER IS A WEAPON.
EVERY CLICK MATTERS.

N rton
from symantec.

A Call to Victory: Marching into the Future of Guerrilla Marketing

On the Guerrilla Marketing battleground, the quest for creative supremacy is a constant struggle.

As soldiers in this relentless war, we must be prepared to face challenges and overcome obstacles in our quest for victory.

As we reflect on these glorious examples of Guerrilla Marketing, we are reminded that strategy, boldness and tenacity are the pillars of achievement. Like a committed army, we must move forward with determination, adapting to changes in battle and seeking new tactics to triumph.

These iconic campaigns are our inspirational generals, brilliant commanders who show us the way forward. They remind us that in a world saturated with information and distractions, we need to find ways to stand out, to command attention in an impactful and unforgettable way.

Like a troop in the making, we must stay on top of emerging trends, using new technologies and approaches to gain an advantage over our competitors. Future Guerrilla Marketing battlegrounds will be shaped by artificial intelligence, virtual reality, social media and other tools we must master to achieve victory.

Our strategy is not limited to the brilliance of creativity, but also to strategic analysis and the meticulous study of the terrain we walk on. We must understand the context in which we find ourselves, identify seasonal opportunities and assess risks to avoid pitfalls and ambushes.

In this ceaseless warfare, remember that perseverance is an invaluable virtue. Not all battles will be won, but each defeat teaches us valuable lessons and makes us stronger. Learn from your failures, adjust your strategy, and be ready to rise and fight again.

Soldiers, the future of Guerrilla Marketing is in our hands. It is our duty to move forward with courage, creativity and relentless determination.

With each campaign, each innovative idea, we move one step closer to victory.

So, raise your war flag, sharpen your strategic skills and march bravely into the future of Guerrilla Marketing.

Our customers, our brands and our reputation are at stake. May creativity be our weapon and innovation be our shield.

Soldiers, forward! Victory is within reach, and together we will conquer the world of Guerrilla Marketing.

Who is Matheus Martins Soares?

 Matheus is an Ex-Military / Presidential Agent, graduated in Marketing since 2018 and specialist in copywriting. He has written for more than 27 different niches, showing his ability to adapt to different topics and audiences. Throughout his career, he has worked in large companies, such as the largest business magazine in the country and the largest marketing consultancy in Brazil. Contributed to the success of important campaigns, generating + 30mm in sales for its customers. Published over 100 books on Amazon and gained readers in over 10 different countries. An expert in StoryTelling and UX Writing, he also works behind the scenes as a GhostWriter, giving voice to other people's ideas and stories. His method is capable of writing a book in less than 24 hours.

With a strategic vision and knowledge in marketing, he helps companies, authors and literary projects to achieve success. He found himself in the world of marketing, writing and human behavior, his ability to adapt to different challenges is a differential that makes him stand out in his field.